Iconic Tattoo

Richard Harries

Stairwell Books //

Published by Stairwell Books
161 Lowther Street
York, YO31 7LZ

www.stairwellbooks.co.uk
@stairwellbooks

ISBN: 978-1-913432-56-0
p8

Layout design: Alan Gillott

Cover art: Jim Danby

Also by Richard Harries

Awakening

Dedicated to Barry Dale, Andrew Goer, Richard Kenn and Julian Wilson. All of whom were lovely young people and good friends who died before they were 21 and are not forgotten.

Table of Contents

Iconic Tattoo

A young man, a physio
At the hospital helping me
After hip replacement
Lots of extraordinary tattoos
Beautiful, expensive, striking indeed
On his right inner arm
A large image from wrist to elbow
A beautiful lady
I looked twice, seemed familiar
An iconic image of Twiggy
In Pierrot costume from the 'Boyfriend' film
I thought, well, it couldn't be, could it?
He was in his twenties
He'd not know who Twiggy was, would he?
So, being me, I asked who it was
'Some bird from the 60s'
So Twiggy it was, dominating his arm
And he had never heard of her
I told him about her and her recent fame
As the stylish mature woman in the M & S ads
How strange but wonderful
That such an iconic image survives
To be worn with pride and the young man?
Well he was interested and off home to Google Twiggy
Then came a surprise
As the icon in the New Year became a Dame
Wonder if the young physio knows? ⁄⁄

The Tattoo

'I'm not sad anymore'
Said the plaque
Held by the cute cartoon bird
Tattooed on the young man's arm
I never know if it's rude and intrusive
To read messages
Tattooed on people's bodies

But, if they don't want you to read
The words and illustrations
Why have them put there so prominently
In such bright colours and large letters?

Being me
Of course
I asked him why
It was there

'Oh, I'm in a band
And it's one of my songs'
Was the reply
And knowing the people I know
That made perfect sense!

Now where should I place
AWAKENING and ICONIC TATTOO? ✍

Friendship Hotel

Friendship is like a hotel
Some check in and are mean
Negative, determined to complain,
Toxic. Cut them out
Refuse to let them book in again

Others check in briefly
Would never be staying long
But fun, happy people
Enjoy them while you can
Even if you know they won't book a return

Then there are those that arrive
And they are there for a long time
Nurture them and have fun with them
They may not be there for ever
And things and circumstances change
Enjoy them while they are booking in

Then there are the lifers
The true friends
The ones that are there for you
Have fun with you
But when you need them
They are always there
In good times and in bad
Let them book in lifelong
And count yourself fortunate
That they are there //

The Confusion of the Rose

I am confused
Things are strange
I sleep most of the year but in June I bud
Then bloom
With my flowers beautiful
Full of colour and fragrance
Then my petals fall and I return to sleep
This has been my fate for centuries
Life is good and regular usually

In recent years
I stir and am disturbed
My buds develop in spring, in autumn
And even in winter
I feel so odd
Flowering amidst frost
Sleet and especially snow
What has happened to the world?
What has caused this madness?
These are not halcyon days
Life and the planet has changed
Something has altered the climate
The planet itself
It's not the plants
It's not the birds and the beasts
The only other being I know
Is humankind
It can't be their fault
This disorder

Can it? ⁄⁄

Good Intentions

Now I know my woman well, I am able to buy for her just
swell
I know what jewellery she likes,
That's courage you say ... yikes!
So yesterday I went into town and did not buy her a gown
No I saw a blouse and a stole, that matched, and it is my
goal
To try to please my beloved wife, and be thoughtful
throughout life
So I did what many men have not the courage to do
But looked at the sizes and I knew
That they would fit my beloved one
And I did what I knew I should have done
I went inside that charity shop
And did buy both of these great tops
Now this was at great inconvenience to me
As I could not now buy the food intended for tea
In fact I would have to make a second trip to the shop
To get enough vegetables for me to chop
So that we could eat fresh food
And have a lovely tea so good
But this I was quite prepared to do
Looked forward to the appreciation and praise that I was due

I got home and showed them off proudly
She to me did exclaim loudly
'Oh my! Just why?'
And she said with a sigh
'You should not have paid cash
It was rather daft and rash
But oh why? Did you buy
These tops, they are complete flops'
'Go on tell me why'
Said I with a sigh

'Well last Friday I donated them
Not wanting to wear them again
You were with me that day
When I gave them away
And last but not least
Of all
You have the gall
To not have noticed that I'
And again she did sigh
'Have worn then for the last four years
Honestly you could drive me to tears!'

All I could say was 'oops and wow!'
'I kind of remember then now!' ⁄⁄

The Shadow Box

As she lay dying
She looked up and saw
The shadow box of her life
The little things that mattered
The first ornament her boy had made at school
A souvenir from the seaside
Tiny shiny things
Nothing of value

Her life had been good and long
She had memories to look back on

She sighed and breathed her last

Time stood still
Then the house was cleared
Memories gone

And the shadow box?
Sadly.... on a bonfire smouldering

Then gone ⁄⁄

The Weathered Old Tree

The willow weeps
And weeps and weeps
It's vast and wide and high and old

The house it stands by is high and old
It is weathered
Has been there so long

The willow weeps and reaches up
And is as high
As the high, high house

How long has it been there
Years and years
Decades, eons maybe?

So very long
Such a long time ago
Way back when no one can say?

The house it looks old
Weathered like the tree
Seems to have been there so long

Not so, because one day
When I was at school
I walked past the new, new house

I saw a man trying to plant a tiny, tiny tree
And he called to me
And asked me to hold the tiny, tiny tree

While he filled in the hole
And firmed up the ground
And ensured it would grow

It was a tiny, tiny tree
And when I went past the other day
It had become vast, as vast as can be

It made me think of my life
It seems to have been so brief
Yet I must be old, older than the tree

Like that great big tree
Like the weathered old house
Weathered, weathered me! ✐

Inspired by Downtown

This has been written as Part 3 of the group of poems set in
Harrogate in 'Awakening'

Loneliness was mine
Had left home
Well been thrown out
Plenty of worries
College in the day
Work at night to pay the bills
No help or support from anywhere
So just an empty bedsit to return to
No phone, so isolated

A record player on the floor
No plug on, just bare wires into socket
A fawn and red Dansette
Albums Melanie, Joni, Aretha
Motown and especially Petula
And I was so alone I played them all
And realised that to forget all my troubles and cares
I should go into the town
And meet folk there

I knew a place in Harrogate
On Montpelier it was, a cellar bar
Can't remember the name
Plenty of music
No bossa nova but did hear the traffic on the way
Lights outside in the trees
Not neon but bright enough for me

There was music and beer
Friendly faces and folk to talk to
I did not need to be alone
I was indeed Downtown
Had taken Petula's advice
Had found a place to go
It was indeed a friendly, safe home ⁄⁄

George Stinney

I was researching injustices and came across this case which moved me to tears

In 1944, which seems so long ago
But it is within my sister's lifetime
And just eight years before I was born
In America, the land of the free
A 14 year old Black boy was executed
For the murder of two little girls
He was placed in the electric chair
Had to be seated on a large bible
Used as a booster seat he was so small
The girls were battered to death
Their bodies were dumped in a ditch
The boy was George Stinney
He had spoken to them that day as they passed his house
He directed them to where they could pick certain flowers
That is all that was proven
He was arrested and taken from his parents
Allowed no solicitor
Even though the Sixth Amendment guarantees him one
Allowed no visits from his family
They could not agree on the description of the murder weapon
And there was no blood found on George
At the trial his council was a white politician
Campaigning for election
In a town full of hatred
Where lynching was threatened
He cross examined no one
George was alibied by his sisters
Which they still swear is the truth

Yes this is so close in time that some of the witnesses are
Still alive
The trial, just 81 days after the murders
Lasted one and half hours, the all white jury were out ten
minutes

1,000 whites packed the courtroom
Not one Black person allowed in
George was not allowed to see his parents until after his
conviction
In America, the Land of the free
At the trial they allowed discussion of rape and even
necrophilia
Even though post mortems pronounced the girls to be virgins
The trial papers have 'disappeared'
As has an alleged confession
One made by a 14 year old boy deprived of contact
With parents or counsel
They killed him with a too large hood that allowed the
tears flowing to be seen
His Dad was allowed to approach and speak to him just
before he died
The only family contact he had had since his arrest
This was in 1944, in America
He was buried in an unmarked grave
70 years later the conviction was overturned
For lack of evidence and for being tainted with racism
They never found the murder weapons.
How could a child hide metal objects so thoroughly? He
could not.
A real murderer ran free.
While they murdered another child.
This was in America
George died because he was Black
If anyone can't comprehend why Black Lives Matters
Why we need to take the knee
They should research George Stinney

No one says other lives do not matter
What they say in America in particular
There is good reason to fear your early death
If you are Black
And that should never have been
And can no longer be ⁄⁄

Dust and Rubble

First published by Editions Oxbia (France)
A short film about a young Ukrainian woman moved me to tears

The film started
A young woman came into view
Dressed in anorak and wooly hat
Walked up to a stunning white piano
She flexes her fingers
She takes her seat
Brushes the dust and rubble
Away from the keyboard

So sad, I am in floods of tears
So sad, how can this be?

She starts to play and is magical
Passion and creative genius flow
As the music from her heart and soul
Pours from her fingers, so beautiful
The piano is her baby, you can tell
She loves it so much
The camera pans to the floor
Rubble and debris everywhere

So sad, I am in floods of tears
So sad, how can this be?

We see the home in disarray
Broken doors lying in heaps on the floor
Dust and debris in a cared for home
Artwork still hanging on the walls
The music flows on as we watch in horror
The invasive destruction of a family home
The message is clear
She is leaving today, leaving all behind

So sad, I am in floods of tears
So sad, how can this be?

Her piano will be left
Amidst the rubble and dust
Her cherish and loved possession
Will probably be destroyed
The tragedy of this hits me so hard
I am utterly floored
This is futile but utter loss
Loss of her of life

So sad, I am in floods of tears
So sad, how can this be? ⁄⁄

Spanish Flu

Written in lockdown 2020. First published in the White Rose Anthology 2022.

World War 1 has always moved
And fascinated me
A vast tragedy on such a huge scale
Families and communities decimated
A generation of young men annihilated
Whenever I read or studied about it
I often saw that afterwards many were killed
By the Spanish Flu
Did not register greatly
Not full of action and trenches
No Man's Land and blood

It was a pandemic

50 million died

50 million who had just been bereaved

50 million isolated and confused

No TV or radio to inform them
No call boxes
Phones were only for the rich
No Community hubs, mobile phones
Google, computers

Just terror and illness and death

Having lived through the strain of this pandemic
I wonder at their strength to survive at all
I am horrified for them
And ashamed I did not comprehend what they went
through ⌀

To My Mother

Written during the first lockdown 2020 at the height of the stress

Hello Mum
Oh OK you don't like Mum or Mother or Ma
So it's Mummy
Hello Mummy
You have been gone now for 57 years but we still think of you
You died at 50
So long ago

We are now the older generation
Judi died at 49 so did not even have as much time as you
Sue and Meg and I are now the old ones
Yes I know they were Susan and Margaret but things change
I am still Richard though (but have been Rick and Dick in my time)

You had grandchildren, lots of them
And they had kids too
So now you are a Great Grandma
And we worry about the children
Like you worried about us

Now we live in a strange world
A world where a pandemic rules
And Mummy, we are frightened
Angry, bewildered, scared
I woke up this morning
And had to write to you ⁄⁄

Bedtime Accident

Dedicated to Naomi Swinden and Jennifer Bailey to whom this happened

Now sweet Jennifer went to bed
'Goodnight Mummy' to Naomi she said
Went straight to sleep
In slumberland so deep
Then woke with a start
And with a thudding heart
Felt something nasty all over her
She wanted her Mummy near
So she called out
And did shout
'There's something all over me
It's all brown and nasty I can see'

Naomi went fast to her room
She saw Jennifer was filled with gloom
She thought it was sickness or worse
Did smile and refuse to curse
As she mopped it away
As Jennifer just wanted to lay
And go back to sleep
Ever so deep
The problem now was Mr Tickle her toy
That Jennifer cuddled with joy
He was so old it would be bold
To put him in a washing machine
Which would destroy him would be mean

Then Naomi saw wrappers of gold
Covered in brown mess not cold
And she realised Grandma's treat
Of chocolate coins, a sort of sweet
Had been taken to bed by mistake
And had melted into a chocolate lake
So Jennifer had not been ill at all
And only into liquid chocolate did fall
Mr Tickle when washed was as good as new
And Naomi was relieved and sighed 'phew' ⁄⁄

17

Beautiful Me

I am so lucky me
I am so attractive
Sexy
And I am now 70
Still have that great appeal
I know this must be so because
On Facebook so often I have young
Beautiful and often bare breasted women
Asking to be my friend
And it's all because of my great looks
And sex appeal
They tell me so
They say they want
Yes they want
To have sex
With me, yes sex

At first it was mainly from Asia
But now it's from everywhere
They tell me they want to meet me
All it will take is me to send them the money for the flight
Or even just my bank details
I must have greatly improved with age
As I did not have this problem in my twenties
Women crawling all over me
To get at my body
And it's not just my body they are after
They have seen my kind eyes
Looked into them and have seen my generous soul
They have had their villages destroyed by hurricane
Or by volcanic eruptions
And they know I will pay to rebuild them

They just googled SEXY MAN

Now not being totally stupid
Nor yet having dementia
I block the bastards
Cos not only will they be thieves after my cash
But they also might be male, 80,
Syphilitic and called Stan

Of course things can go wrong
As a friend got such a friend request
From a woman he did not know
Pretty and smiling
So blocking seemed to be the way to go
Turns out it was his step sister's daughter
Who he had not seen for years
Whoops
If only he was not also so damned attractive ✐

We Could Not Help Him
Dedicated to my friend David Hart

We saw him as he stumbled forward
He moved again
And jerked
Shook all over
Staggered backwards and his spine arched
His legs kicked out
Seemingly uncontrollably
There was light shining into his eyes
They were glazed
He twisted violently and awfully
Seemed out of control
What was happening?
His head jerked
There was sweat glistening on his face
There was another lurch forward
His shoulders now hunched grotesquely
As he swayed on his feet unsteadily
We all looked on aghast
How terrible was this?
What could we do?
He was out of control
We had no means of help
Could we do anything at all?
No
There was nothing we could do
Helpless
It was hopeless
Dreadful
Well was there no remedy for this
Did we just have to stand and watch
In slow motion
As this awful event unfolded?
Horror
And it seemed to last forever
The three-minute frenzy ended
Peace

The noise gone
He relaxed
Walked off the dance floor
And Dave's dreadful embarrassing uncle at a wedding
dance
Was over! ⁄⁄

We All know a Pinocchio

We all know one
Tell lies but not for fun
Lie through their teeth
No rhyme or reason but all the time
So wearying if they are in your life
Could not cope if it was my wife

There are some where if I ask the time
Or what it's like outdoors
I would pause and check
For they lie without cause
In every respect

But without respect for you

Most folk lie to get out of trouble
Or get someone else into crap
Or to gain reward
Or promotion
To shift blame elsewhere

A Pinocchio lies for no reason
Could be cos they want to be liked
They don't know if they did not invent stories
And bull themselves up
All the time
That they might be liked
For themselves

But it's so tiring
Checking
And disbelieving all the time
That really pisses me off

Don't know why they are like this
But they are
And it's not fine
Not all the time

So wearying //

Parisienne Encounter

We went to Paris to see Petula Clark
Arrived at noon so it was not dark
Eileen was unpacking her stuff and mine
So I decided to use my time fine
Off I went to a Parisienne Bar
Just round the corner not too far
To have a Cognac was my idea great
Found a quaint bar and did relax and wait

Now, we had been warned that in the district of the hotel
The ladies of the night plied their trade well
Surely not a problem just now?
Until an incident occurred and this is how

An elderly lady, rather like Madame Edith in ALLO ALLO
Dealt my self esteem an incredible blow
I thought that at 40 I was a young lad
To find out this was not so was sad

She must have been well over 70 years of age
And still working, wanting a living wage

She smiled at me
As warmly as can be
How very sweet I thought
Then she brought me up short

'Bonjour monsieur, Ca va bien?'
'Ca Va' said I, as politely as I can
I beamed at her cos she was friendly like a gran
But after she spoke again – I ran!

'TU VEUX L'AMOUR?'
Oh my God the gran was a whore!

'PAS MAINTENANT' I did say
Which kind of means 'but later in the day'

She beamed at me again and I did flee
Shot into the hotel now a sanctuary for me

Up to our room, Eileen was startled as I crashed in
Looking bright red and panicky with no grin
I told her what had happened that day
And swore never again would I wander away ⁄⁄

Reflections of a Georgeian Doll

Dedicated to friend Susan Marsden who requests this poem every time she attends a reading by me. This poem won 1st prize in a NORTHERN POETRY competition on Facebook

I was loved
I truly was
I know I was
I was adored
Played with so gently
Treated so very carefully

I have long hair that can be dressed
I have a gorgeous panelled dress
With beauty I am blessed

Once my girl had gone to bed
I was placed on a shelf and heard stories read
Tales of the king, the German George
And of his marriage to his cousin Sophia, so flawed
I heard of wars, I heard of affairs of love
I heard piano playing sweet enough to be the cooing of a
dove

I am clothed in silk and lace
And have bisque for my hands, feet and face
Through the years my girls had their own girls
I had even more love and care unfurled
I always heard the news
Napoleon did his wars rue
Jane Austen wrote such romantic books
Charles Dickens wrote about villainous crooks
Wordsworth, Shelley and Byron came to my ears
Slavery was abolished ending so many fears
Victoria ruled an Empire so vast
I understood it would forevermore last
I heard of the trenches of the Great War
And saw soldiers returning crippled and sore

Then suddenly my world went black
I stood silently wondering when my life would come back
One day I was discovered in a loft so dark
And was held so gently so as to not leave a mark
I was placed in a special case
With glass to the front so you could see my face
I was taken to a museum so fine
And now the glory of display is mine
Talk about my age
And my value seems to be the rage
But as I stand and watch the crowds go by
I wish that to one of my girls I could fly
With their ringlets and posies, so full of grace
Now the girls seem to have metal piercing in their face
The sweeping gowns have gone away
And jeans and miniskirts have their way

No one seems now to be bright and fresh
And from here I can see far too much flesh!

Oh I long for an evening in my home
And to a museum I would never roam
The harpsichord and the pianoforte
Seem so much gentler than the music today

Please Lord let me have one more caress
I'd do anything to return to one of my girls I do confess ⁄⁄

What Happened in a Field

She lay there exposed in the sun
Spread wide having such fun
The breeze stimulated her delicate surface
She was waiting for his wonderful embrace
He approached in a state of much excitement
His senses in a state of high enlightenment
He was excited at seeing her there
Unveiled in her beauty aloof and bare
He quivered and smelt her beautiful scent
She attracted him he knew what that meant
She was glowing with colour and waved at him
He did not think what he was about to do was sin
He hovered around her drinking her in
She was so lovely, fine and thin
She had everything he needed there
There was nowhere else he'd rather be, nowhere
She was so beautiful seemed so perfect to him
Fulfilled his every need to the brim
When he was ready he entered her there
He needed the loveliness and only for her did he care
Once inside he felt he was in heaven indeed
She was supplying his every need
He felt her touch on his bare back
She really knew what she was doing, she had the knack
How glad he was that she had been in the field
So that to him she could readily yield
He moved around and had a great time
Collecting the pollen that was just fine
He had freed the nectar from that lovely flower
And left to take his treasure his hive to endower
I trust that you realised at once that he was a bee
And she, a lovely big red wild poppy! ⁄⁄

The Time of Their Lives

Inspired by a beautiful Christmas card depicting Victorian skaters

The Snow Queen had frozen all
The ground was hard
The river ran solid
Victoria was on the throne
And the Thames was frozen

He got out his skates
His top hat
His warm clothes
He went down to the river

And to the time of his life

She brushed her long hair
Well, her maid did that
And dressed her warmly and carefully
She got out her skates
Went down to the river
And to the time of her life

Elegance and decorum were the order of their age
Chaperones abounded
Morals were astounded
Offended and abrogated
By anything that did not conform
To strict rules

As he flew across the ice
She did too, their eyes met
The love was instant
Hopeless, helpless

They knew in that moment they had found true love
In that instant was the time of their lives

The Snow Queen
Had brought them together
In their passion
And elegance

Luckily for them in that age
They shared a heritage and standing
So they could marry
And have the time of their lives
For the rest of their lives ⁄⁄

A Man and a Woman

A modern version of the traditional English Folk Song OXFORD CITY

They lay there
Sated
In the afterglow of
Farewell sex

He was desolate
He loved her
And needed her
She was moving on

He had asked her
Time and again
To marry him
She had said no

This last time
That they
Would be together
Was her Farewell

It was killing him
He was desolate
She was going
His was an unrequited love

To love like this
And not be loved in return
Was dreadful
Awful. Heart breaking.

'But I do love you
It's been fun
And the sex was great'
She had said

'We have had fun
We need to move on
I love you
But when you're not there
I don't miss you
Don't need you there
You are not the reason I live
You are not THE one'

That tore him apart
As she WAS the one
For him
All he needed

'A glass of wine
Before you go my love
A farewell drink
And off you go?'

He smiled and she agreed
Thinking of tomorrow
When she would pack
And go to university
And start the rest of her life

They raised their glasses and drank
A sweet final kiss
Then she stood up
Felt dizzy
And staggered

'What have you done?'
She cried
He looked at her with love
'Yes I poisoned the wine
If I can't have you
Then no one will'

She cried

And lay there and he lay too
'I also have drunk the wine'
I will join you
And for eternity
We will be together'

And then they died ⁄⁄

A Sad Tale of Woe

I was so excited
I started as a sack
But now my life is blighted
Now everything is off track
They gave me arms and legs
Then stuffed my sack with straw
They made my fingers with pegs
I was so proud, became a boor

I boasted of how fine I looked
My trousers seemed so grand
On my appearance I was hooked
But I stood not on rock but sand
For I was hoping to be a scarecrow
Standing proud in a field
But my fate has been a real blow
And to my future I yield

I have found out what that is
And it's not good, oh my
For sadly I have found out, oh gee whiz
That my name is GUY
To be taken to a farmers field
And placed upon a pyre
That is my fate to which I yield
And to be set on fire! ⁄⁄

Husband and Wife Talking

This happens in our house every time we have visitors to stay

Oh my God
Our daughter's coming to stay
And she is arriving today
With her husband and kids
Oh my God
We have to clean

No we don't

We have to clean
And tidy away, fill the fridge
Dairy free, lactose free, gluten free too
Fill the cupboards as well

No we don't

Oh tidy everything on the table
Change the lampshades
Dust the... well everything
Put the dirty washing out of sight
Only pure cotton sheets on every bed

No we don't

Oh put things in the shed
Weed the flower bed, prune the hedge and mow the lawn

Again?

Wash the kitchen floor
Dust the TV
Sweep the front path

It's clean

Oh don't be a bore

We'll do it again
Hang blackout blinds
Fill dishes with fresh fruit
Bake a cake

We'll be fine

Vacuum all the floors
Wash the kitchen cupboard doors
Should we paint the garden wall?

They're coming to see us not the house

I know who will win
So I'll now shut up and grin

And then she arrived
Emptied the car
Dumped the trammell for four
Put the girls to bed
Sat and relaxed

And then smiled
And said
'Lovely to see you both'
And sighed
'Why isn't the white wine cold in the fridge?'

Prem Baby

The sperm shot out
As sperm do
Swam fast
And direct
Got to the egg
Implanted itself
And started a life
A miracle
Who would know how long this life would last
And what it would achieve?

The pregnancy was bad
A terrible time
And short term
A tiny, prem baby
A sickly one
With tubes and a long time in the incubator
Months before the little boy could be taken home
So tiny and frail
With three boisterous older sisters

Convulsions were the next nightmare
But they passed
Then the family moved from London to Cairo
And the baby nearly died
Scarlet fever and then Diphtheria
More lengthy periods in hospital, in the heat
A scary time for all
So much love for him
Especially from his frightened mother

As time went by there were more health problems
Glandular fever, whooping cough, pneumonia
But the child managed to thrive and overcome all this
Got married became a Dad

Were the health problems connected to the premature birth?
Some research says so
But we will never know
How will the story end?
Well I am not at the end of the journey yet
Have more recently survived diabetes, a new hip and cataracts
It is all ongoing

So I do not know the end yet ⫽

Humankind

Humankind is clever
Oh so clever
It rules the world
So well
The greatest engineering project ever
In the world, they said
Railway
Eternal, a lasting achievement
Till in England they closed so many lines
Canals were allowed to clog up
They now dig them out
Replace removed tramlines

Inventions?
Oh yes so clever
Like nylon, fleece and lycra
Lasting so well
So cheap and so much profit
But everytime they are washed
They release microfibers into the sea, polluting them

Humankind is so clever
Inventing durable never ending plastic
And with it they cover the planet
No other species leaves such waste
Every other living being
Leaves only bodily waste, biodegradable

Oh humankind is so clever
Mobile phones and other items to plug into the ears
Causing deafness, more folly
Microwaves, largely untested
Humankind invented built in obsolescence
Convenient for the manufacturers but not the consumers
So many mistakes while being clever

Additives leading to allergies and conditions
So maybe humankind is not so clever

And I have not mentioned power, control and corruption
And of course war ⁄⁄

That Top Hat

Originally published by the Silver Birch Press

I was twelve
Yes twelve
The youngest of four
My sister got married

I was a thin
Lanky
Twelve year old
I was put into
A top hat
Yes a top hat
And tails

I felt
An utter prat
Yes a prat
This was the sixties
I was meant to be swinging
Not stood around like a geek

I was tall
Nearly six foot
Did I mention I was lanky?
Well how tall did I feel
In a top hat?
Shiny
Top hat
And with those tails!

It is so long ago
Yet I remember it still
And when hats are mentioned
I return to that
Very memorable day
Instantly! ⁄⁄

The Hat Speaks

Written to follow THAT TOP HAT *as a result of a challenge by fellow poet and friend Ross Punton*

I am used to being hired out
I grace extremely superior heads

I am after all a 7 ¾
Not small enough for a child

I am worn with respect
I am treated well

My wearers drink champagne
Nibble caviar
And their deportment is perfection

Can you imagine my horror then
When one day in 1964
I was hired out with my brothers
And I was put on the head of a lanky child?

He kept taking me off and fidgeting
He RAN around, he even sang out loud
He was so silly
I mean dropping me on the grass
And leaving me on chairs
Where I could have been squashed

In all my years at weddings
I have never before been
So scared, really scared and ashamed
I still have nightmares about that day //

The Slim Fit Shirt

First published by the Silver Birch Press
This follows a six stone deliberate weight loss

I bought a slim fit shirt
Yes!
Me!

I bought a slim fit shirt
It fit!
It did!

The buttons did up
And did not gape
On my slim fit shirt
Slim fit!
Mine!

I bought a slim fit shirt
OK
It was a large slim fit shirt
But
It was the first slim fit shirt I had bought
Since
Well
Let me think

OK
I bought a slim fit shirt
For the first
Since
Like Well
EVER!

I bought a slim fit shirt! ⫽

Mother Nature Nurtures (1)

The heat was scorching
10 months since rain last fell
Walked through woodland

Dead trees
Ready to fall
Bare earth
No vegetation
Just litter
Rocks, stones
Brackish dead plants
Would burst into flame easily
Desolation, sterility and death

Returned five months later
After replenishing rain
Same woodland ablaze with flowers
Masses of greenery
Could not see the rocks, the stones or the litter
Trees that had seemed dead?
Mimosa in bloom
The scent amazing
No bare earth showing
So many vibrant colours
Nature had worked its miracle
The urge to survive, to live had won through
Miraculous indeed ✍

Mother Nature Nurtures (2)

Dry
Scorched
Dead
Barren
After so much sun
We left, returned after rain
A mass of colour
Lush greenery
Mimosa in bloom
Nature had miraculously survived, and thrived ⁄⁄

Three Sisters

It was an innocent time
Three young ladies so fine
So well to do
Looking serenely out at you
What was in their future... who knew?
They said there would soon be a war
Over by Christmas 1914 they foresaw

But now

Before anything had happened
They went to the photographic studio
In their Sunday best
Posing so formally
So their unity would be
Remembered for all time
Their youth and beauty would be preserved
Such splendid dresses
Meticulous hair
And such distinctive
And refined
Jewellery
What a day!
Life was for them and theirs
They lived and loved
Married, gave birth, grew old
And died

I suppose

Happiness and tragedy were theirs
Two World wars
A way of life disappeared

And then

They were forgotten
As if they never were
Someone's great great grandmothers

And the photograph so carefully posed for?

I found it for a pound in a charity shop ⁄⁄

Music Makes Me Feel

It actually makes me feel
Alive inside
It makes me feel good
Makes me feel sad
It reaches every part of me
Music enters my heart
My soul
My being
Can transport me back in time
To warm place
To my inner child
To happy times dancing through life
Or to the saddest of times
To my mother's arms

60 years ago
To a holiday camp aged 10
Having fun
It can make me cry
Bring joy
Be cathartic
Music is universal
It's in my head and heart
All the time
In a dentist's chair
I turn it on in my head
It carries me through the bad
Love it
Can't do
Won't do
Without it
Ever //

Queen Concert, Elland Road, 1982

Occasionally I have luck
Good luck
And Fortune smiles on me
In 1982 I was given a task
Paid good money
Very good money
Overtime
In fact double time
And a day of in lieu
What was my task so grim?
Security at a concert
At Elland Road
A rock concert sold out
A stadium gig
Packed full of peaceful music lovers
Who wanted to see and hear
Freddie!
The great Freddie, with the rest of Queen!

The Teardrop Explodes, Joan Jett and Heart
Were wonderful indeed
But they were obliterated
The moment Freddie pranced on stage
To the strains of 'FLASH! Uh huh'
Explosions and lights lit his way up and on
Scaffolding erected as he sang
His charisma
Dimmed all else

I had no work to do
As he transfixed the crowd
There may have been a certain mild scent in the air
But no trouble
No violence
As he rocked with

Fat Bottomed Girls
Bo Rap and so many more
It was the time of my life
A halcyon day indeed
No rowdiness
As people gave themselves to his genius and beauty
All revelled in his talent
That voice
That presence
The athlete in him
The wonder that was Freddie

He was surrounded by greatness as he rocked you
Loved you
Bit the dust with you
And was your champion
The rest of the band complemented him
And Brian, with his big hair
Was magnificent
Oozing genius and charisma too

A great day
So many memories
I was truly blessed

The world is so much richer
For having had Freddie in it
And I am blessed for having been there
That wonderful night! ⧸⧸

On David Bowie Passing

So he had a new album out
Causing a fuss
Getting rave reviews
And a new single
That was a huge success already too

He has been around so long
Always changing
Re-inventing
Always making comebacks
When he had never actually been
Away

My first memory of him is Major Tom
Startling on Top of the Pops
So many brilliant things
Through the decades
He has truly touched the lives of millions
And been adored
His music will last eternally
He will remain adored

Unique
No one like him
An ever changing chameleon
Visually
Artistically
Musically

I got up late
Overslept
Turned on the TV
Phillip Schofield sat there
Looking sad
A picture of Bowie

Illuminating the screen

'Oh His album's No 1
Is it?'
I thought
And then the words announcing
His death came
I could not comprehend this
I had been expecting a tour
My brain would not accept
This dreadful news
It took a long time
For the words to sink in
And for me to accept
This tragedy, a man to be mourned the world over
Leaving us far too soon ⁄⁄

I Heard Sam Cooke Sing!

I have always had music
Around
In my life
In my head
As a child I heard lovely sweet singers
In Disney films
We had Snow White on 78s
I watched songbirds on TV (only the BBC back then)
They stood still and sang
The only Black artist I saw
Was Winifred Atwell
Resplendent in her gowns
And sparkling jewellery
As she played her piano
And inspired Elton John

Then one day at a holiday camp
I heard a sound, a record
A sound that kind of exploded in my head
It moved, it grooved
It thundered, it lived inside me
It changed the way I listened
Perceived
It was profound
Sam Cooke

I could not put a name to it
I now know it to be soul
And it entered my soul
Sam thundered out CUPID
And this experience
Changed the way I heard things
And was profound

Sam left us far too soon
You never know if those that do
Would have gone on to achieve more
But with Sam, and Otis and Buddy
You just know they would have
Continued with their genius
The tragedy of his mysterious death
Robbed the world of so much
Cut short with violence
Many claim he was murdered

Sam you were indeed
No you still are the main man
The King of Soul
The one who Aretha and Otis followed
As Beyoncé followed them
And are still adored
And a profound influence
And will remain so ⁄⁄

Tina Turner Concert 1960s

It was in the sixties
Quite early on in my memory
Had music in my head - still do
I saved my pocket money for records
Vinyl records
And to see concerts
Live

I was about 14
Loved soul music so much
And to sleepy Harrogate town
Came a revue
Ike and Tina Turner with the Ikkettes
I knew I IDOLISE YOU and A FOOL IN LOVE
Don't remember if RIVER DEEP had arrived then or not
A funny thing the memory

I was used to sweet
Calm English singers
Who stood in a spotlight
And sang their songs straight

Ike was stunning, brilliant
Majestic with his guitar
The Ikettes stormed on
And dazzled chanting away

Then Tina exploded on stage
Prancing and dancing
Skimpy clothing
Like I had never seen
Sort of things only a Flintstone woman wore
In a cartoon of fun but this was not fun
This was the sexiest thing I had ever seen
And that long black hair, long below her waist

Was flying around everywhere
She was a dancer, a rhythmic athlete
A gymnast indeed
Lights coloured the stage
Explosions of mist at her feet
I was stunned

She sang her heart out
Entranced us, everyone went wild
I left the concert
At the good old Harrogate Royal Hall
Speechless
Yes, me speechless
I just could not speak
Have seen many great artists
In the years since then
But Tina poleaxed me
In a way no other has since

They returned twice more
As I recollect
Each time as great
By then I had bought the albums
And knew what to expect
That first concert is in my memory
And the emotions I felt
Stun me still ⁄⁄

1964, 1975 and 1996

Massive Petula fan, as some of you may know
Have been since I was four
The only person to be on THIS IS YOUR LIFE
In UK three times

In 1964, aged 12 was in the bath
I like baths
Still do
When my Mum shouted up the stairs
'THIS IS YOUR LIFE Petula Clark'
I ran dripping in a towel and watched it enthralled
Remember Jack Warner and Kathleen Harrison
Being so sweet

The time passed
Grew up, married
1975, aged 23 was in the bath
I love baths, really
When my wife shouted up the stairs
'THIS IS YOUR LIFE Petula Clark'
I ran dripping in a towel and watched it enthralled
Remember The Carpenters, at the height of their fame
Being so sweet

Then in 1996 aged 44 was in the bath
I do, I really love baths
Got out dripping
Dried myself and went to watch THIS IS YOUR LIFE
Friend Mike had been at the theatre
When they surprised her again
Rang and warned me, so this time I knew!
Remember Don Black
Saying 'you live your songs'

Each show was lovely and had Anthony Newley there
Being loving and supportive
A lifelong friend of hers
Made films as kids
She not only endures in her career
But this lovely lady does make friends for life ⁄⁄

Two Boys

Dedicated to Barry Dale

Two boys
Played in the street, had fun
Laid a foundation stone
For a new church
Posed with their trowels in the sun

Went to school together
Had fun, grew older
Off to senior school
At 14
One went on the rugby pitch
Ran, tackled, collapsed, died

Had a heart condition
That no one knew about
He never made 21
Had no more fun

I am 70, I am the other boy
The church is now weathered and old
As I am

I have had so much fun
That's not fair
So why did I survive? ⁄⁄

Life's Tapestry

The boy stands still in time
His yesterday was his alone
No one had had his life
And he felt secure within the past

Today was troubling
What to do next?
How would he decide?
Where would he go?

Tomorrow was frightening
What would his journey be?
Where would he settle?
With whom, and why?

Then suddenly the years had past
And he knew where he had ended up
Not in perfection but not despair
Life's tapestry had woven its spell ⁄⁄

Bracelets and Buttocks

Odd the glimpses of life you see
Of passing strangers
On a coach trip behind two women
One holds her phone with a bright lit screen
Attracts my attention in the dark
Scrolls down, a lot
Likes jewellery, a lot
Looks at gold jewellery
40 % off, clicking a lot to buy
Then between the bracelets
Buttocks, naked buttocks
Male buttocks, a lot
Didn't really get to know her
But when I think of that trip
I think of her and bracelets and buttocks, a lot ⁄⁄

Damp, Misery and Glamour

In the glamour and the rush
Of the West End theatre crowds
Socialising and happy
£85 tickets, money well spent
A glittering shop, the window ablaze with light
Bejewelled basques and teddies
Tutus resplendent with net and glitter
Such extravagance and lavishness
£300, £400 and even £500
Frivolity and merriment

In the well-lit doorway
In front of these displays
A young homeless lad
With a thin, damp blanket
Shivering away ⁄⁄

Proposal

Look in the mirror
In the pub toilet
Feel fear
Unease
Fingers through hair
Flatten it
Straighten T-shirt
Walk towards door
Sweating
Nervous
Repeat process
Several times
Come out to her smile
Her beautiful dark eyes
And hair
Navy blue and white
Dress
With lattice across her breasts

Chat
While my head inside thunders
And I try to keep my nerve
To form my words
She senses my struggle
Is uncertain
Nervous
Wonders what is coming
We drink
Drink some more
Leave pub
And walk on dark unlit road
Nerves thunder
Stop outside old building
She looks at me in the darkness
As I go down on one knee
And tell her I love her
Ask her to be my wife ⁄⁄

Bless Her

She fell badly
At swimming pool
Alarm
Paramedics
Neck and back braces
Ambulance, blue light job
Pilgrim Hospital
Strapped to a trolley
Waiting
Eternally waiting
Doctor came
She indicated to him
Laid there, cold
Strapped down still
'Doctor I'm worried'
So was I. Terrified.
He leant forward
Said 'What is it?'
Looked concerned
'My husband he's diabetic and
He's missed his lunch
He should have carbs...'

Bless her ⁄⁄

I Wish

Sing
To granddaughters
About them, about me
'Grandpa is wonderful'
'Isabel are you well?'
'Lara Rose wriggle your toes'
Sing old children's songs
Little Shoemaker
And the like
Play Petula on YouTube
Christopher Robin
Little Blue Man
YouTube goes on
To Downtown
Another I sing to them
Often
'Oh Grandpa
Does the lady sing this too?
We thought it was one of yours'

I wish! ⁄⁄

Real People

A civic reception
In Norfolk, Virginia
The Arts Festival in full flow
Petula headlining
Had been invited
We went inside
Awaited her arrival
Drinks in hand
In she came
Spoke to the officials
All lined up
Including the Mayor and
The President of the Festival
She turned, looked at us
'Ooh real people
I didn't know real people would be here'
Moved forward, delighted
And kissed Eileen, my wife //

South Norwood Suite
Dedicated to my amazing and beloved Aunty Marg

Roly Poly Days

I used to visit family in the south
Travelled on a train all that way
Norwood Junction bound
We climbed an apple tree
In the back garden
And then many times
We went to Shirley Hills
Ah, Shirley Hills
I see in my memory
Slopes and leaves
Trees and bracken
Brambles and fun!
We climbed the slopes
And lay in the leaves
No thoughts of health and safety then
We rolled down the slope
Over and over, faster and faster
Then climbed back up and rolled again
Roly poly what a childhood game
What joy and fun
I must have been scratched and bumped
But what sweet memories

Train Fright

Staying with an aunt
Near Croydon
Aged 14, maybe
With my cousin and her cousin
Went by train to London
Visit shops, museums
Maybe a theatre
Got in carriage

One with a compartment, set off
Rolled down window
Stuck out head
Pulled back violently
By my cousin's cousin
As train passed close
Going other way
Scared the living daylights out of me
Could have been a short life

My First Curry

The Tower of London, aged 10
Full of wonder
The vastness and majesty of the place
With dear aunt and cousin
Aunt always treated us, spoilt us
Having seen amazing things
And thought of poor Anne Boleyn
And Catherine Howard
Emerged and saw on pavement
A street vendor selling CURRY AND RICE!
I asked for some, please
'Do you like curry?' said Aunty in surprise.
This was 1962, curry was unknown, exotic
'Yes' I lied like kids do
I wanted it, no idea what it was
But it was steaming and I was cold
There were queues for the curry
Must be good
Now I'd never had curry
And thought pepper was hot
Aunty Marg bought it, cousin Rosemary stuck to her ice
cream
I looked at the container, I smelled it
Then got the fork, took a scoop
Popped it in my mouth

My head exploded
My mouth did too
Thought I'd lost my teeth
Cried, tears running down my cheek
Snot pouring out
I gagged
And decided this was death

After everything calmed down
And Aunt and cousin has stopped crying with laughter
And I had eaten an ice cream
Fast
I decided that
Maybe, just maybe
I should never again
Lie to a dear, sweet Aunt!

Tinned Pineapple

My beloved Aunty Marg
So sweet and loving
The centre of our family
The one that kept us together
So that decades after she died
We are still in touch, we visited her every Easter
She knew we did not have too many treats
Pop. Fizzy pop. Unknown to us.
Tinned pineapple we had never seen
We loved it and begged for it
So she reacted as sweet Aunty Marg would
Tinned pineapple with every meal nearly every meal
We had so much tinned pineapple
That now if I see it I always think of her
And sadly rarely eat it, cos we had so much then

A Tree in Suburbia

A cherry tree lined road
In Spring such lovely blossom
Gardens to the rear
In one an apple tree
A big, fun apple tree
Branches reached high
We climbed it, swung from it
Laughed and played
It became the Faraway tree
I had a saucepan on my head
Cousins had so much fun
For many hours, sweet memories

A Special Place

Pink cherry blossom
On Court Road, South Norwood
Number 19, our home from home
Felt safe and loved
Once we turned the corner and saw those trees
That blossom
Sad that I never go now, maybe one day
A final trip down a beloved memory lane //

I Met a Babe...

My granddaughter Lara Rose was born amidst heavy snow and we were unable to travel to see her for weeks. Zooming holding a baby is not the same.

I met a babe in a big old public house
Cute with dark hair – quiet as a mouse
Did Eileen mind that I fell deeply in love?
Not at all, the babe was as lovely as a dove

When I tell you her name is Lara Rose
With twinkling eyes and a sweet little nose
Then you will agree that this abundant love
Is just the sort that poets speak so sweetly of

The overwhelming feeling of love so grand
That grandparents have takes them to a new land
Where all past problems and life's rich strife
Makes you say – IT'S A WONDERFUL LIFE! ⁄⁄

Other anthologies and collections available from Stairwell Books

For further information please contact rose@stairwellbooks.com

www.stairwellbooks.co.uk
@stairwellbooks